Emerging Faith

⌘

Lenten Devotions

Edited and compiled

by Dr. Jeffrey P. Johnson

EMERGING FAITH LENTEN DEVOTIONS
Edited and compiled by Dr. Jeffrey P. Johnson

Cover design by Erin Newton

ISBN 0-89267-293-9

© 2009
(Revised May 2009)
For Men's Ministries International
By Light and Life Communications
Indianapolis, Indiana
Printed in the U.S.A.

BIO

The Reverend Dr. Jeffrey P. Johnson is the Superinten-
dent of Mid-America Conference of the Free Methodist
Church. He has served the Lord 22 years as a pastor and
missionary. As Executive Director for Men's Ministries
International, he travels around the world teaching on
evangelism and discipleship. He serves Butterfield
Memorial Foundation, World Methodist Council Executive
Committee, Wesley Commission, FMCNA Board of
Administration and Central Christian College of Kansas. His
wife, Yasmin, is a Professor of Nursing at Oklahoma Baptist
University, and they have two children, Ian Wesley and
Isabella Anna Pauline.

Jeff has traveled throughout Asia as well as living in
China for three years. He conducts Schools of Discipleship
for churches who are interested in making disciples and
promoting community renewal. He has ministered in more
than 60 countries and over sees works in Guatemala and the
Middle East.

Jeff earned a BA in History and a MA in Education from
Oral Roberts University and a Doctorate in Spiritual
Formation from George Fox Evangelical Seminary.

Web site: MMIfm.org
e-mail: MMIFM@fmcna.org

Men's Ministries International, Inc.
PO Box 535002
Indianapolis IN 46353-5002
800.342.5531 — 317.244.3660

INTRODUCTION

Faith must penetrate not only the mind but the heart as well. The early church learned to walk by faith and in the process helped to define Christianity. Their faith emerged from a firsthand experience with Jesus Christ and was passed on to the next generation through their witness and their testimony. Their emerging faith can be described in two ways. First, faith is a set of doctrines, beliefs or convictions that disciples hold to be true. Second, faith is trust, and disciples learn to relate to God in terms of a personal commitment. This interactive relationship starts with faith: Disciples believe that Jesus is Lord and *feel* God's love through Christ. They move from feelings of insecurity, punishment, hopelessness and rejection to a place where they can feel the love of God. It is in this experience of God that disciples find salvation. They stay with Christ and make their home in him. Jesus described this movement to his disciples in the Gospel of John (John 15:4-8). He said:

"Remain in me, and I will remain in you. No branch can bear fruit by itself; it must remain in the vine. Neither can you bear fruit unless you remain in me.

"I am the vine; you are the branches. If a man remains in me and I in him, he will bear much fruit; apart from me you can do nothing. If anyone does not remain in me, he is like a branch that is thrown away and withers; such branches are picked up, thrown into the fire and burned. If you remain in me and my words remain in you, ask whatever you wish, and it will be given you. This is to my Father's glory, that you bear much fruit, showing yourselves to be my disciples."

Not only do disciples make their home in Christ, but also they feel loved and feel a part of something bigger and better. They can go on to be fruit in the kingdom of God and find the joy God has already given.

The goal of faith is to bring salvation to the soul. This salvation includes holiness and wholeness in Jesus Christ. As disciples live and move in Christ, they discover that faith is re-creating them into the image of God. The re-creation is the start of spiritual formation, and the image of God in Christ is the end of the formation process. It is faith that moves disciples and sets them free. It is faith that survives the undulation of tests, trials and tribulations. It is faith that keeps disciples close to the heart of God. A childlike faith goes a long way in the kingdom of God, and every disciple must exercise his or her faith in the formation process.

ASH WEDNESDAY

Justified By Their Faith

A few days later, when Jesus again entered Capernaum, the people heard that he had come home. So many gathered that there was no room left, not even outside the door, and he preached the word to them. Some men came, bringing to him a paralytic, carried by four of them. Since they could not get him to Jesus because of the crowd, they made an opening in the roof above Jesus and, after digging through it, lowered the mat the paralyzed man was lying on. When Jesus saw their faith, he said to the paralytic, "Son, your sins are forgiven."
Mark 2:1-5

And we, too, being called by His will in Christ Jesus, are not justified by ourselves, nor by our own wisdom, or understanding, or godliness, or works that we have wrought in holiness of heart; but by that faith through which, from the beginning, Almighty God has justified all men; to whom be glory for ever and ever. Amen.
Clement of Rome
c. 96 A.D.

Clement of Rome is listed as the third bishop in the first-century Roman Church, possibly following after Peter and Paul. It is also possible that he is the disciple mentioned in *Philippians 4:3*, as a fellow worker with the Apostle Paul in proclaiming the gospel. The only literature from Clement of Rome is a letter of instruction to the Corinthian Church dealing with dissention and order, and a sermon on living a holy life. In both the letter and the sermon Clement issues a call to repentance and encourages Christians everywhere to serve God in humility, always remembering that it is God Who justifies humanity through their faith in Jesus Christ.

THURSDAY AFTER ASH WEDNESDAY

The Mighty Power of God

"Why are you thinking these things? Which is easier; to say to the paralytic, 'Your sins are forgiven,' or to say, 'Get up, take your mat and walk'? But that you may know that the Son of Man has authority on earth to forgive sins ... ' He said to the paralytic, 'I tell you, get up, take your mat and go home.'" He got up, took his mat and walked out in full view of them all. This amazed everyone and they praised God, saying, 'We have never seen anything like this!'"
Mark 2:8b-12

Let us consider, beloved, how the Lord continually proves to us that there shall be a future resurrection, of which He has rendered the Lord Jesus Christ the first-fruits by raising Him from the dead. Let us contemplate, beloved, the resurrection which is at all times taking place. Day and night declare to us a resurrection. The night sinks to sleep, and the day arises; the day [again] departs, and the night comes on. Let us behold the fruits [of the earth], how the sowing of grain takes place. The sower goes forth, and casts it into the ground; and the seed being thus scattered, though dry and naked when it fell upon the earth, is gradually dissolved. Then out of its dissolution the mighty power of the providence of the Lord raises it up again, and from one seed many arise and bring forth.

Clement of Rome
c. 96 A.D.

The early church took great hope in the resurrection of Jesus Christ. Clement's writings also reveal the state of the ministry during this time, the history of the church in Rome and a testimony to martyrdoms of Peter and Paul.

FRIDAY AFTER ASH WEDNESDAY

Running the Race

Therefore, since we are surrounded by such a great cloud of witnesses, let us throw off everything that hinders and the sin that so easily entangles, and let us run with perseverance the race marked out for us.
Hebrews 12:1

As citizens, they share in all things with others, and yet endure all things as if foreigners. Every foreign land is to them as their native country, and every land of their birth as a land of strangers. They marry, as do all [others]; they beget children; but they do not destroy their offspring. They have a common table, but not a common bed. They are in the flesh, but they do not live after the flesh. They pass their days on earth, but they are citizens of heaven. They obey the prescribed laws, and at the same time surpass the laws by their lives. They love all men, and are persecuted by all. They are unknown and condemned; they are dishonoured, and yet in their very dishonour are glorified. They are evil spoken of, and yet are justified; they are reviled, and bless; they are insulted, and repay the insult with honour; they do good, yet are punished as evil-doers. When punished, they rejoice as if quickened into life; they are assailed by the Jews as foreigners, and are persecuted by the Greeks; yet those who hate them are unable to assign any reason for their hatred.
A Letter to Diognetus from a Disciple
c. 110 A.D.

A short letter by an unknown disciple that encourages Christians to live out their faith with perseverance. The writer stresses that Christians are a hidden presence for the good of humanity.

SATURDAY AFTER ASH WEDNESDAY

Overcoming Faith

This is love for God: to obey his commands. And his commands are not burdensome, for everyone born of God overcomes the world. This is the victory that has overcome the world, even our faith. Who is it that overcomes the world? Only he who believes that Jesus is the Son of God.
1 John 5:3-5

"For whosoever does not confess that Jesus Christ has come in the flesh, is antichrist"; and whosoever does not confess the testimony of the cross, is of the devil; and whosoever perverts the oracles of the Lord to his own lusts, and says that there is neither a resurrection nor a judgment, he is the first-born of Satan. Wherefore, forsaking the vanity of many, and their false doctrines, let us return to the word which has been handed down to us from the beginning; "watching unto prayer," and persevering in fasting; beseeching in our supplications the all-seeing God "not to lead us into temptation," as the Lord has said: "The spirit truly is willing, but the flesh is weak."
Polycarp
c. 69-155

Polycarp was the bishop of Smyrna and is a link between the Apostles and the early church. Several pieces of literature are attributed to Polycarp, including letters to and from him. He was a defender of the faith and even made a trip to Rome to discuss the timing of the Passover festival and the celebration of the resurrection of Christ. Polycarp is one of the few early church writers who claims his conversion through the Apostle John and meeting with others who had seen the risen Christ. He was arrested and martyred during a public pagan festival in Smyrna.

FIRST SUNDAY OF LENT

Keeping the Faith

For I am already being poured out like a drink offering, and the time has come for my departure. I have fought the good fight, I have finished the race, I have kept the faith. Now there is in store for me the crown of righteousness, which the Lord, the righteous Judge, will award to me on that day — and not only to me, but also to all who have longed for his appearing.
2 Timothy 4:6-8

"Now, as Polycarp was entering into the stadium, there came to him a voice from heaven, saying, 'Be strong, and show thyself a man, O Polycarp!' No one saw who it was that spoke to him; but those of our brethren who were present heard the voice. And as he was brought forward, the tumult became great when they heard that Polycarp was taken. And when he came near, the proconsul asked him whether he was Polycarp. On his confessing that he was [the proconsul] sought to persuade him to deny [Christ], saying, 'Have respect to thy old age,' and other similar things, according to their custom, [such as], 'Swear by the fortune of Caesar; repent, and say, Away with the Atheists.' But Polycarp, gazing with a stern countenance on all the multitude of the wicked heathen then in the stadium, and waving his hand towards them, while with groans he looked up to heaven, said, 'Away with the Atheists.' Then, the proconsul urging him, and saying, 'Swear, and I will set thee at liberty, reproach Christ; Polycarp set thee at liberty, reproach Christ'; Polycarp declared, 'Eighty and six years have I served Him, and He never did me any injury: how then can I blaspheme my King and my Saviour?'"

The Martyrdom of Polycarp
c. 155 A.D.

MONDAY, FIRST WEEK OF LENT

Opening the Door

Those whom I love I rebuke and discipline. So be earnest, and repent. Here I am! I stand at the door and knock. If anyone hears my voice and opens the door, I will come in and eat with him, and he with me. To him who overcomes, I will give the right to sit with me on my throne, just as I overcame and sat down with my Father on his throne. He who has an ear, let him hear what the Spirit says to the churches.
Revelation 3:19-22

"O Lord God Almighty, the Father of thy beloved and blessed Son Jesus Christ, by whom we have received the knowledge of Thee, the God of angels and powers, and of every creature, and of the whole race of the righteous who live before Thee, I give Thee thanks that Thou hast counted me worthy of this day and this hour, that I should have a part in the number of Thy martyrs, in the cup of thy Christ, to the resurrection of the eternal life, both of soul and body, through the incorruption [imparted] by the Holy Ghost. Among whom may I be accepted this day before Thee as a fat and acceptable sacrifice, according as Thou, the ever-truthful God, hast fore-ordained, hast revealed beforehand to me, and now hast fulfilled. Wherefore also I praise Thee for all things, I bless Thee, I glorify Thee, along with the everlasting and heavenly Jesus Christ, Thy beloved Son, with whom, to Thee, and the Holy Ghost, be glory both now and to all coming ages. Amen."
The Martyrdom of Polycarp
c. 155 A.D.

This testimony was written by a disciple from the church in Smyrna as a witness to Polycarp's faith and love in Christ.

TUESDAY, FIRST WEEK OF LENT

Seeking Life

For to me, to live is Christ and to die is gain. If I am to go on living in the body, this will mean fruitful labor for me. Yet what shall I choose? I do not know! I am torn between the two: I desire to depart and be with Christ, which is better by far; but it is more necessary for you that I remain in the body.
Philippians 1:21-24

All the ends of the world, and all the kingdoms of this earth, shall profit me nothing. It is better for me to die for the sake of Jesus Christ, than to reign over all the ends of the earth. "For what is a man profited, if he gain the whole world, but lose his own soul?" I long after the Lord, the Son of the true God and Father, even Jesus Christ. Him I seek, who died for us and rose again. Pardon me, brethren: do not hinder me in attaining to life; for Jesus is the life of believers. Do not wish to keep me in a state of death, for life without Christ is death. While I desire to belong to God, do not ye give me over to the world. Suffer me to obtain pure light: when I have gone thither, I shall indeed be a man of God. Permit me to be an imitator of the passion of Christ, my God.

Ignatius of Antioch
c. 107

Ignatius was bishop of Antioch and was martyred for his faith in Jesus Christ. While he traveled to Rome he wrote letters to churches and individuals about his impending death.

WEDNESDAY, FIRST WEEK OF LENT

Immovable Faith

Remember Jesus Christ, raised from the dead, descended from David. This is my gospel, for which I am suffering even to the point of being chained like a criminal. But God's word is not chained. Therefore I endure everything for the sake of the elect, that they too may obtain the salvation that is in Christ Jesus with eternal glory.
2 Timothy 2:8-10

I glorify God, even Jesus Christ, who has given you such wisdom. For I have observed that ye are perfected in an immoveable faith, as if ye were nailed to the cross of our Lord Jesus Christ, both in the flesh and in the spirit, and are established in love through the blood of Christ, being fully persuaded with respect to our Lord, that He was truly of the seed of David according to the flesh, and the Son of God according to the will and power of God; that He was truly born of a virgin, was baptized by John, in order that all righteousness might be fulfilled by Him; and was truly, under Pontius Pilate and Herod the tetrarch, nailed [to the cross] for us in His flesh. Of this fruit we are by His divinely-blessed passion, that He might set up a standard for all ages, through His resurrection, to all His holy and faithful [followers], whether among Jews or Gentiles, in the one body of His Church.

Ignatius of Antioch
c. 107

This comes from Ignatius' letter to the church in Smyrna where Polycarp was the bishop. There are several versions of his letters with most scholars agreeing on the seven longer versions. Ignatius also wrote several shorter letters, including one to the Virgin Mary.

THURSDAY, FIRST WEEK OF LENT

Signs of Life

While they were still talking about this, Jesus himself stood among them and said to them, "Peace be with you." They were startled and frightened, thinking they saw a ghost. He said to them, "Why are you troubled, and why do doubts rise in your minds? Look at my hands and my feet. It is I myself! Touch me and see; a ghost does not have flesh and bones, as you see I have."
Luke 24:36-39

For I know that after His resurrection also He was still possessed of flesh, and I believe that He is so now. When, for instance, He came to those who were with Peter, He said to them, "Lay hold, handle Me, and see that I am not an incorporeal spirit." And immediately they touched Him, and believed, being convinced both by His flesh and spirit. For this cause also they despised death, and were found its conquerors. And after his resurrection He did eat and drink with them, as being possessed of flesh, although spiritually He was united to the Father.

Ignatius of Antioch
c. 107

Ignatius was taken to Rome under the guard of 10 soldiers and was found guilty of treason. Several people pleaded for his release, but Ignatius kneeled and prayed for all the churches. The emperor immediately had him thrown into the coliseum, and he was devoured by wild beasts. His remains were wrapped in linen and returned to Antioch to be buried in the church where he was converted and ordained. Ignatius believed that his love for Christ and his good confession of his faith would be a testimony to the churches of his time and a witness for Christians everywhere.

FRIDAY, FIRST WEEK OF LENT

Walking in the Light

This is the message we have heard from him and declare to you: God is light; in him there is no darkness at all. If we claim to have fellowship with him yet walk in the darkness, we lie and do not live by the truth. But if we walk in the light, as he is in the light, we have fellowship with one another, and the blood of Jesus, his Son, purifies us from all sin.
1 John 1:5-7

The way of light, then, is as follows. If any one desires to travel to the appointed place, he must be zealous in his works. The knowledge, therefore, which is given to us for the purpose of walking in this way, is the following. Thou shalt love Him that created thee: thou shalt glorify Him that redeemed thee from death. Thou shalt be simple in heart, and rich in spirit. Thou shalt not join thyself to those who walk in the way of death. Thou shalt hate doing what is unpleasing to God: thou shalt hate all hypocrisy. Thou shalt not forsake the commandments of the Lord.

Barnabas of Alexandria

c. A.D. 125

The letter of Barnabas of Alexandria was written to encourage Gentile Christians not to make the same mistakes as the Jewish religious leaders did in their interpretation of Holy Scripture. He encourages them to avoid observances and trifle interpretations that lead to conflict and disunity. He encourages them to walk in the light of the Lord and to learn that God's love conquers all. He concludes his letter by calling Christians everywhere "children of love and peace."

SATURDAY, FIRST WEEK OF LENT

Word Made Flesh

In the beginning was the Word, and the Word was with God, and the Word was God. He was with God in the beginning. Through him all things were made; without him nothing was made that has been made. In him was life, and that life was the light of men. The light shines in the darkness, but the darkness has not understood it. The word became flesh and made his dwelling among us. We have seen his glory, the glory of the One and Only, who came from the Father, full of grace and truth.
John 1:1-5, 14

Our doctrines, then, appear to be greater than all human teaching; because Christ, who appeared for our sakes, became the whole rational being, both body, and reason, and soul. For whatever either lawgivers or philosophers uttered well, they elaborated by finding and contemplating some part of the Word. But since they did not know the whole of the Word, which is Christ, they often contradicted themselves.
Justin Martyr
c. 100-165

Justin Martyr was born in Samaria and converted to Christ at the age of 30 after studying various philosophies. He is famous for debating with Trypho the Jew in Ephesus and later opened a Christian school in Rome. He wrote his first defense (first apology) of Christianity to the Emperor Antonius Pius and his second defense (second apology) of Christianity to the Roman Senate. Justin was arrested and refused to sacrifice to the emperor. He was sentenced to be scourged and beheaded. Justin Martyr believed in the "germinative" Word, which means that God has sown the seed of truth in all people. God then sent Christ into the world to be the Word made "flesh," and thus teach the whole truth in the redemption of humanity.

SECOND SUNDAY OF LENT

Worship

They devoted themselves to the apostles' teaching and to the fellowship, to the breaking of bread and to prayer. Everyone was filled with awe, and many wonders and miraculous signs were done by the apostles.
Acts 2:42-43

And on the day called Sunday, all who live in cities or in the country gather together to one place, and the memoirs of the apostles or the writings of the prophets are read, as long as time permits; then, when the reader has ceased, the president verbally instructs, and exhorts to the imitation of these good things. Then we all rise together and pray, and, as we before said, when our prayer is ended, bread and wine and water are brought, and the president in like manner offers prayers and thanksgivings, according to his ability, and the people assent, saying Amen; and there is a distribution to each, and a participation of that over which thanks have been given, and to those who are absent, a portion is sent by the deacons. And they who are well to do, and willing, give what each thinks fit; and what is collected is deposited with the president, who succours the orphans and widows, and those who, through sickness or any other cause, are in want, and those who are in bonds, and the stranger sojourning among us, and in a word that takes care of all who are in need. But Sunday is the day on which we all hold our common assembly, because it is the first day on which God, having wrought a change in the darkness and matter, made the world; and Jesus Christ our Saviour on the same day rose from the dead.

Justin Martyr
c. 100-165

Taken from Justin Martyr's "The First Apology" to the Roman Emperor.

MONDAY, SECOND WEEK OF LENT

Word of Faith

But what does it say? "The word is near you; it is in your mouth and in your heart," that is, the word of faith we are proclaiming: That if you confess with your mouth, "Jesus is Lord," and believe in your heart that God raised him from the dead, you will be saved. For it is with your heart that you believe and are justified, and it is with your mouth that you confess and are saved. As the Scripture says, "Anyone who trusts in him will never be put to shame." For there is no difference between Jew and Gentile — the same Lord is Lord of all and richly blesses all who call on him, for, "Everyone who calls on the name of the Lord will be saved."
Romans 10:8-13

And I replied, 'I do not say so; but those who have persecuted and do persecute Christ, if they do not repent, shall not inherit anything on the holy mountain. But the Gentiles, who have believed on Him, and have repented of the sins which they have committed, they shall receive the inheritance among the patriarchs and the prophets, and the just men who are descended from Jacob, even although they neither keep the Sabbath, nor are circumcised, nor observe the feasts. Assuredly they shall receive the holy inheritance of God.

Justin Martyr
c. 100-165

This comes from a debate with Trypho, a Jewish theologian. In the text Trypho asks questions on which Justin responds using mostly the prophet Isaiah. At one point Trypho asks Justin why he uses only Isaiah, to which Justin replies that Isaiah directly points to the coming of the Messiah, which Justin declares is Jesus of Nazareth.

TUESDAY, SECOND WEEK OF LENT

Raised in Power

So will it be with the resurrection of the dead. The body that is sown is perishable, it is raised imperishable; it is sown in dishonor, it is raised in glory; it is sown in weakness, it is raised in power; it is sown a natural body, it is raised a spiritual body. If there is a natural body, there is also a spiritual body. So it is written: "The first man Adam became a living being"; the last Adam, a life-giving spirit. The spiritual did not come first, but the natural, and after that the spiritual. The first man was of the dust of the earth, the second man from heaven.

1 Corinthians 15:42-47

If He had no need of the flesh, why did He heal it? And what is most forcible of all, He raised the dead. Why? Was it not to show what the resurrection should be? How then did He raise the dead? Their souls or their bodies? Manifestly both. If the resurrection were only spiritual, it was requisite that He, in raising the dead, should show the body lying apart by itself, and the soul living apart by itself. But now He did not do so, but raised the body, confirming in it the promise of life. Why did He rise in the flesh in which He suffered, unless to show the resurrection of the flesh? And wishing to confirm this, when His disciples did not know whether to believe He had truly risen in the body, and were looking upon Him and doubting, He said to them, "Ye have not yet faith, see that it is I."

Justin Martyr
c. 100-165

In Justin's "First Apology" he gives a brief account of early church baptisms and communion. Faith in the Resurrection plays an important part in these holy sacraments.

WEDNESDAY, SECOND WEEK OF LENT

Free Indeed

Jesus replied, "I tell you the truth, everyone who sins is a slave to sin. Now a slave has no permanent place in the family, but a son belongs to it forever. So if the Son sets you free, you will be free indeed."
John 8:34-36

But this is our Lord, the Word of God, who in the first instance certainly drew slaves to God, but afterwards He does Himself declare to His disciples: "I will not now call you servants, for the servant knoweth not what His lord doeth; but I have called you friends, for all things which I have heard from my Father I have made known." For in that which He says, "I will not now call you servant," He indicates in the most marked manner that it was Himself who did originally appoint for men that bondage with respect to God through the law, and then afterwards conferred upon them freedom. And in that He says, "For the servant knoweth not what his lord doeth," He points out, by means of His own advent, the ignorance of a people in a servile condition. But He terms His disciples "the friends of God."

Irenaeus
c. 130-200

Irenaeus was the bishop of Lyons and heard Polycarp when he was a young boy. He studied in Rome and became a pastor of Lyons and after some fierce persecution became a bishop of Lyons in 177 A.D. Irenaeus became one of the first theologians of the church by opposing Gnosticism, emphasizing the elements of worship, and canonizing what he thought were the letters for the New Testament including the authority of the four Gospels.

THURSDAY, SECOND WEEK OF LENT

Submit

Submit yourselves, then, to God. Resist the devil, and he will flee from you. Come near to God and he will come near to you. Wash your hands, you sinners, and purify your hearts, you double-minded. Grieve, mourn and wail. Change your laughter to mourning and your joy to gloom. Humble yourselves before the Lord, and he will lift you up.

James 4:7-10

But if the servant say in his heart, "The Lord delayeth, and begin to beat his fellow-servants, and to eat, and drink, and to be drunken, his Lord will come in a day on which he does not expect Him, and shall cut him asunder, and appoint his portion with the hypocrites." All such passages demonstrate the independent will of man, and at the same time the counsel which God conveys to him, by which He exhorts us to submit ourselves to Him, and seeks to turn us away from the sin of unbelief against Him, without, however, in any way coercing us. No doubt, if any one is unwilling to follow the Gospel itself, it is in his power to reject it, but it is not expedient. For it is in man's power to disobey God, and to forfeit what is good; but such conduct brings no small amount of injury and mischief. And on this account Paul says, "All things are lawful to me, but all things are not expedient."

Irenaeus

c. 130-200

Irenaeus was an important connection between the Greek church and the Latin church. Copies of his letters and sermons can be found in at least four ancient languages. One of his best works is titled "Apostolic Preaching," which encourages young pastors to use notable Old Testament passages for preaching.

FRIDAY, SECOND WEEK OF LENT

The Perfect Everything

In the past God spoke to our forefathers through the prophets at many times and in various ways, but in these last days he has spoken to us by his Son, whom he appointed heir of all things, and through whom he made the universe. The Son is the radiance of God's glory and the exact representation of his being, sustaining all things by his powerful word.

Hebrews 1:1-3a

And as He was the servant of God, so is He the Son of God, and Lord of the universe. And as He was spit upon ignominiously, so also did He breathe the Holy Spirit into His disciples. And as He was saddened, so also did He give joy to His people. And as He was capable of being handled and touched, so again did He, in a non-apprehensible form, pass through the midst of those who sought to injure Him, and entered without impediment through closed doors. And as He slept, so did He also rule the sea, the winds, and the storms. And as He suffered, so also is He alive, and life-giving, and healing all our infirmity. And as He died, so is He also the Resurrection of the dead. He suffered shame on earth, while He is higher than all glory and praise in heaven; who, "though He was crucified through weakness, yet He liveth by divine power;" who "descended into the lower parts of the earth," and who "ascended up above the heavens"; for whom a manger sufficed, yet who filled all things; who was dead, yet who liveth for ever and ever. Amen.

Irenaeus

c. 130-200

Irenaeus of Lyons is a transitional figure in Christian history connecting the church fathers with third-century Christianity.

SATURDAY, SECOND WEEK OF LENT

Affirmation of Faith

Beyond all questions, the mystery of godliness is great: He appeared in a body, was vindicated by the Spirit, was seen by angels, was preached among the nations, was believed on in the world, was taken up in glory.
1 Timothy 3:16

The Church, though scattered through the whole world to the ends of the earth, has received from the Apostles and their disciples the *faith in one God, the Father Almighty,* who made the heaven and the earth, and the seas, and all that in them is; and in one Christ Jesus, the Son of God, *who became flesh for our salvation;* and in the Holy Ghost, who through the prophets preached the dispensations and the advent, and *the birth from the Virgin,* and *the passion,* and *the resurrection from the dead,* and the bodily *assumption into heaven* of the beloved Christ Jesus, our Lord, and his *appearing from heaven* in the glory of the Father, to comprehend all things under one head, and *to raise up all flesh of all mankind,* that, according to the good pleasure of the Father invisible, every knee of those that are in heaven and on the earth and under the earth should bow before Christ Jesus, our Lord and God and Saviour and King, and that every tongue should confess to him, and that he *may execute righteous judgment over all;* sending into eternal fire the spiritual power of wickedness, and the angels who transgressed and apostatized, and the godless and unrighteous and lawless and blasphemous among men, and granting *life* and immortality and *eternal glory* to the righteous and holy, who have both kept the commandments and continued in his love, some from the beginning, some after their conversion.

Irenaeus
c. 130-200

A confession of faith used by Irenaeus of Lyons.

THIRD SUNDAY OF LENT

Abounding Love

And this is my prayer: that your love may abound more and more in knowledge and depth of insight, so that you may be able to discern what is best and may be pure and blameless until the day of Christ, filled with the fruit of the righteousness that comes through Jesus Christ — to the glory and praise of God.
Philippians 1:9-11

For from Faith arises Self-restraint; from Self-restraint, Simplicity; from Simplicity, Guilelessness; from Guilelessness, Chastity; from Chastity, Intelligence; and from Intelligence, Love. The deeds, then, of these are pure, and chaste, and divine. Whoever devotes himself to these, and is able to hold fast by their works, shall have his dwelling in the tower with the saints of God. Then I asked her in regard to the ages, if now there is the conclusion. She cried out with a loud voice, "Foolish man! Do you not see the tower yet building? When the tower is finished and built, then comes the end; and I assure you it will be soon finished. Ask me no more questions. Let you and all the saints be content with what I have called to your remembrance, and with my renewal of your spirits.

Hermas

c. 160

"The Shepherd" was written by an Apostolic Father named Hermas who was a contemporary of Clement of Rome and is possibly mentioned in Romans 16:14. He was a Christian slave who was set free in Rome. During the time of persecution he lost all his property and was denounced by his own family for his faith in Jesus Christ. Hermas teaches on Christian virtues such as: faith, truth, chastity and love and exhorts Christians to wait for God to deliver them.

MONDAY, THIRD WEEK OF LENT

Doing Good

He saved us through the washing of rebirth and renewal by the Holy Spirit, whom he poured out on us generously through Jesus Christ our Savior, so that, having been justified by his grace, we might become heirs having the hope of eternal life. This is a trustworthy saying. And I want you to stress these things, so that those who have trusted in God may be careful to devote themselves to doing what is good. These things are excellent and profitable for everyone.

Titus 3:5b-8

The angel then said to me, "Conduct yourself manfully in this service, and make known to every one the great things of God, and you will have favor in this ministry. Whoever, therefore, shall walk in these commandments, shall have life, and will be happy in his life; but whosoever shall neglect them shall not have life, and will be unhappy in this life. Enjoin all, who are able to act rightly, not to cease well-doing; for, to practice good works is useful to them. And I say that every man ought to be saved from inconveniences. For both he who is in want, and he who suffers inconveniences in his daily life, is in great torture and necessity. Whoever, therefore, rescues a soul of this kind from necessity, will gain for himself great joy. For he who is harassed by inconveniences of this kind, suffers equal torture with him who is in chains.

Hermas

c. 160

For a time "The Shepherd" of Hermas was considered part of the New Testament canon in place of the Book of Revelation. It is written in an apocalyptic style with visions and judgments from God to the church with warnings and encouragements to those who faithfully hold on until the end.

TUESDAY, THIRD WEEK OF LENT

Looking Forward

Since everything will be destroyed in this way, what kind of people ought you to be? You ought to live holy and godly lives as you look forward to the day of God and speed its coming. That day will bring about the destruction of the heavens by fire, and the elements will melt in the heat. But in keeping with his promise we are looking forward to a new heaven and a new earth, the home of righteousness.

2 Peter 3:11-13

And on this account we believe that there will be a resurrection of bodies after the consummation of all things; not, as the Stoics affirm, according to the return of certain cycles, the same things being produced and destroyed for no useful purpose, but a resurrection once for all, when our periods of existence are completed, and in consequence solely of the constitution of things under which men alone live, for the purpose of passing judgment upon them. Nor is sentence upon us passed by Minos or Rhadamanthus, before whose decease not a single soul, according to the mythic tales, was judged; but the Creator, God Himself, becomes the arbiter.

Tatian of Rome
c. 160

Tatian was from Assyria and was converted in Rome under the ministry of Justin Martyr. He was a strict disciplinarian and left Rome and founded an ascetic sect near Antioch. He was considered to be an apostolic father but also a second-century heretic. Tatian fell under the influence of Gnosticism, which believes that knowledge trumps faith in relationship to God, and in the end believed he was the master of his own destiny. Most scholars believed that Tatian deserves a critical reading to appreciate his relation to the early church.

WEDNESDAY, THIRD WEEK OF LENT

Things Above

Since, then, you have been raised with Christ, set your hearts on things above, where Christ is seated at the right hand of God. Set your minds on things above, not on earthly things. For you died, and your life is now hidden with Christ in God. When Christ, who is your life, appears, then you also will appear with him in glory.

Colossians 3:1-4

Since, then, my friend, you have assailed me with empty words, boasting of your gods of wood and stone, hammered and cast, carved and graven, which neither see nor hear, for they are idols, and the works of men's hands; and since, besides, you call me a Christian, as if this were a damning name to bear. I, for my part, avow that I am a Christian, and bear this name beloved of God, hoping to be serviceable to God. For it is not the case, as you suppose, that the name of God is hard to bear; but possibly you entertain this opinion of God, because you are yourself yet unserviceable to Him.

Theophilus of Antioch

c. 168

Theophilus was the Bishop of Antioch in the latter part of the second century. He wrote three books addressed to a pagan friend named Autolychos explaining the Christian idea of God and defending the doctrine of creation. In his writings Theophilus developed an argument based on the intelligence of the Father and the power of the Word in creation. Theophilus was the first theologian to use Trinitarian language to describe the Godhead. He refers to God the Father, God the Son and God the Holy Spirit, as a "Triad."

THURSDAY, THIRD WEEK OF LENT

Transforming Faith

I always thank my God as I remember you in my prayers, because I hear about your faith in the Lord Jesus and your love for all the saints. I pray that you may be active in sharing your faith, so that you will have a full understanding of every good thing we have in Christ. Your love has given me great joy and encouragement, because you, brother, have refreshed the hearts of the saints.
Philemon 4-7

But far be it from Christians to conceive any such deeds; for with them temperance dwells, self-restraint is practiced, monogamy is observed, chastity is guarded, iniquity exterminated, sin extirpated, righteousness exercised, law administered, worship performed, God acknowledged: truth governs, grace guards, peace screens them; the holy word guides, wisdom teaches, life directs, God reigns. Therefore, though we have much to say regarding our manner of life, and the ordinances of God, the maker of all creation, we yet consider that we have for the present reminded you of enough to induce you to study these things.

Theophilus of Antioch
c. 168

The church in Antioch produced several faithful Christians before Theophilus including Barnabas and Ignatius. In Acts 13:1-3 it says there were prophets and teachers in Antioch who were disciplined and filled with the Holy Spirit. In the early church, Theophilus ranks with Justin Martyr and Irenaeus as defenders of the faith. Unfortunately, there are only three books still in existence that bear Theophilus' expressions of hope and explanations of the truth. He also had an immense knowledge of heathen poetry and philosophy, which he works into his discussions on Christianity.

FRIDAY, THIRD WEEK OF LENT

Son of God

*For God so loved the world that he gave his one and only Son,
that whoever believes in him shall not perish but have eternal life.
For God did not send his Son into the world to condemn the world,
but to save the world through him.*

John 3:16-17

Nor let any one think it ridiculous that God should have
a Son. For though the poets, in their fictions, represent the
gods as no better than men, our mode of thinking is not the
same as theirs, concerning either God the Father or the Son.
But the Son of God is the Logos of the Father, in idea and in
operation; for after the pattern of Him and by Him were all
things made, the Father and the Son being one. And, the Son
being in the Father and the Father in the Son, in oneness and
power of spirit, the understanding and reason of the Father
is the Son of God. But if, in your surpassing intelligence, it
occurs to you to inquire what is meant by the Son, I will
state briefly that He is the first product of the Father, not as
having been brought into existence (for from the beginning,
God, who is the eternal mind, had the Logos in Himself,
being from eternity instinct with Logos); but inasmuch as He
came forth to be the idea and energizing power of all
material things, which lay like a nature without attributes,
and an inactive earth, the grosser particles being mixed up
with the lighter.

Theophilus of Antioch

c. 168

Some of the lost books by Theophilus include *Commentaries on
the Gospels, Chronology of the Life of Christ, Commentaries on
Proverbs* and *Histories on the Old Testament*.

SATURDAY, THIRD WEEK OF LENT

New Creation

If we have been united with him like this in his death, we will certainly also be united with him in his resurrection. For we know that our old self was crucified with him so that the body of sin might be done away with, that we should no longer be slaves to sin — because anyone who has died has been freed from sin.
Romans 6:5-7

And as this follows of necessity, there must by all means be a resurrection of the bodies which are dead, or even entirely dissolved, and the same men must be formed anew, since the law of nature ordains the end not absolutely, nor as the end of any men whatsoever, but of the same men who passed thorough the previous life; but it is impossible for the same men to be reconstituted unless the same bodies are restored to the same souls. But that the same soul should obtain the same body is impossible in any other way, and possible only by the resurrection; for if this takes place, an end befitting the nature of men follows also. And we shall make no mistake in saying, that the final cause of an intelligent life and rational judgment, is to be occupied uninterruptedly with those object to which the natural reason is chiefly and primarily adapted, and to delight unceasingly in the contemplation of *Him who is,* and of His decrees.

Athenagoras
c. 177

Athenagoras is described as the "Christian philosopher of Athens." He is known for defending the doctrine of the Resurrection and explaining how Christians will interact with God in eternity. He also used Trinitarian language for describing God and believed that marriage was indissoluble even after death.

FOURTH SUNDAY OF LENT

Marriage

A woman is bound to her husband as long as he lives. But if her husband dies, she is free to marry anyone she wishes, but he must belong to the Lord. In my judgment, she is happier if she stays as she is — and I think that I too have the Spirit of God.
1 Corinthians 7:39-40

Nay, you would find many among us, both men and women, growing old unmarried, in hope of living in closer communion with God. But if the remaining in virginity and in the state of a eunuch brings nearer to God, while the indulgence of carnal thought and desire leads away from Him in those cases in which we shun the thoughts, much more do we reject the deeds. For we bestow our attention, not on the study of words, but on the exhibition and teaching of actions, — that a person should either remain as he was born, or be content with one marriage; for a second marriage is only specious adultery. "For whosoever puts away his wife," says He, "and marries another, commits adultery"; not permitting a man to send her away whose virginity he has brought to an end, nor to marry again. For he who deprives himself of his first wife, even though she be dead, is a cloaked adulterer, resisting the hand of God, because in the beginning God made one man and one woman, and dissolving the strictest union of flesh with flesh, formed for the intercourse of the race.

Athenagoras
c. 177

The early church believed that procreation was a major purpose of marriage. This then placed an emphasis on virginity, chastity and celibacy.

MONDAY, FOURTH WEEK OF LENT

Common Graces

As a prisoner for the Lord, then, I urge you to live a life worthy of the calling you have received. Be completely humble and gentle; be patient, bearing with one another in love. Make every effort to keep the unity of the Spirit through the bond of peace. There is one body and one Spirit — just as you were called to one hope when you were called — one Lord, one faith, one baptism; one God and Father of all, who is over all and through all and in all.
Ephesians 4:1-6

Let us, then, embracing more and more this good obedience, give ourselves to the Lord, clinging to what is surest, the cable of faith in Him, and understanding that the virtue of man and woman is the same. For if the God of both is one, the master of both is also one; one church, one temperance, one modesty; their food is common, marriage an equal yoke; respiration, sight, hearing, knowledge, hope, obedience, love all alike. And those whose life is common, have common graces and a common salvation; common to them are love and training.

Clement of Alexandria
c. 150-215

Clement of Alexandria was probably born in Athens and studied in Alexandria, Egypt. He became a teacher around the age of 40 but fled during the persecutions of the third century. Clement wrote several works, including an exhortation to the Greeks, a book of Christian life and manners, and several other pieces on faith and logic. Clement presents his theology as a spiritual journey in three steps: the Word of God, the baptism of the believer, and the deification of the disciple.

TUESDAY, FOURTH WEEK OF LENT

A Song for the Savior

Oh, the depth of the riches of the wisdom and knowledge of God! How unsearchable his judgments, and his paths beyond tracing out! "Who has known the mind of the Lord? Or who has been his counselor?" "Who has ever given to God, that God should repay him?" For from him and through him and to him are all things. To him be the glory forever! Amen.
Romans 11:33-36

Bridle of colts untamed, over our wills presiding; wing of unwandering birds, our flight securely guiding. Rudder of youth unbending, firm against adverse shock; Shepherd, with wisdom tending Lambs of the royal flock: Thy simple children bring in one, that they may sing in solemn lays their hymns of praise with guileless lips to Christ their King.

King of saints, almighty Word of the Father highest Lord; wisdom's head and chief; assuagement of all grief; Lord of all time and space, Jesus, Saviour of our race; Shepherd, who dost us keep; husbandman, who tillest, bit to restrain us, Rudder to guide us as Thou willest; of the all-holy flock celestial wing; Fisher of men, whom Thou to life dost bring; from evil sea of sin, and from the billowy strife, gathering pure fishes in, caught with sweet bait of life: Lead us, Shepherd of the sheep, reason-gifted, holy One; King of youths, whom Thou dost keep, So that they pollution shun: steps of Christ, celestial Way; Word eternal, age unending; Life that never can decay; Fount of mercy, virtue-sending; life august of those who raise unto God their hymn of praise, Jesus Christ!

Clement of Alexandria
c. 150-215

Clement was an ordained elder and directed a theological school in Alexandria with Origen being one of his students. His contemporaries referred to him as the "holy Clements."

WEDNESDAY, FOURTH WEEK OF LENT

Faith Seeking Understanding

In fact, everyone who wants to live a godly life in Christ Jesus will be persecuted, whole evil men and impostors will go from bad to worse, deceiving and being deceived. But as for you, continue in what you have learned and have become convinced of, because you know those from whom you learned it, and how from infancy you have known the holy Scriptures, which are able to make you wise for salvation through faith in Christ Jesus. All Scripture is God-breathed and is useful for teaching, rebuking correcting and training in righteousness, so that the man of God may be thoroughly equipped for every good work.

2 Timothy 3:12-17

For many reasons, then, the Scriptures hide the sense. First, that we may become inquisitive, and be ever on the watch for the discovery of the words of salvation. Then it was not suitable for all to understand, so that they might not receive harm in consequence of taking in another sense the things declared for salvation by the Holy Spirit. Wherefore the holy mysteries of the prophecies are veiled in the parables — preserved for those chosen men, selected to knowledge in consequence of their faith; for the style of the Scriptures is parabolic. Wherefore also the Lord, who was not of the world, came as one who was of the world to men. For He was clothed with all virtue; and it was His aim to lead man, the foster-child of the world, up to the objects of intellect, and to the most essential truths by knowledge, from one world to another.

Clement of Alexandria

c. 150-215

Clement fled the persecution of Alexandria and went to Jerusalem to teach Christians and to help pilgrims on their journey of faith. He also traveled to Antioch and died around 215 A.D.

THURSDAY, FOURTH WEEK OF LENT

Faith Alive

Who is going to harm you if you are eager to do good? But even if you should suffer for what is right, you are blessed. "Do not fear what they fear; do not be frightened." But in your hearts set apart Christ as Lord. Always be prepared to give an answer to everyone who asks you to give the reason for the hope that you have. But do this with gentleness and respect, keeping a clear conscience, so that those who speak maliciously against your good behavior in Christ may be ashamed of their slander.

1 Peter 3:13-16

"For the eyes of the Lord," he says, "are upon the righteous, and His ears on their prayers": he means the manifold inspection of the Holy Spirit. "The face of the Lord is on them that do evil"; that is, whether judgment, or vengeance, or manifestation. "But sanctify the Lord Christ," he says, "in your hearts." For so you have in the Lord's prayer, "Hallowed be Thy Name." "For Christ," he says "hath once suffered for our sins, the just for the unjust, that he might present us to God; being put to death in the flesh, but quickened in the spirit." He says these things, reducing them to their faith. That is, He became alive in our spirits. "Coming," he says, "He preached to those who were once unbelieving." They saw not His form, but they heard His voice.

Clement of Alexandria
c. 150-215

Clement of Alexandria left a large invaluable collection of Christian writings, which reveal the ministry and testimony of the early church. His three greatest works are: *The Exhortation,* a book about witnessing to pagans; *The Instructor,* a guide for spiritual formation and Christian character; and *The Miscellanies,* a set of rules and regulations for Christian living.

FRIDAY, FOURTH WEEK OF LENT

Divine Pruning

I am the true vine, and my Father is the gardener. He cuts off every branch in me that bears no fruit, while every branch that does bear fruit he prunes so that it will be even more fruitful. You are already clean because of the word I have spoken to you. Remain in me, and I will remain in you. No branch can bear fruit by itself; it must remain in the vine. Neither can you bear fruit unless you remain in me.

John 15:1-4

In both the commandments, then, He introduces love; but in order distinguishes it. And in the one He assigns to God the first part of love, and allots the second to our neighbour. Who else can it be but the Saviour Himself? or who more than He has pitied us, who by the rulers of darkness were all but put to death with many wounds, fears, lusts, passions, pains, deceits, pleasures? Of these wounds the only physician is Jesus, who cuts out the passions thoroughly by the root, — not as the law does the bare effects, the fruits of evil plants, but applies His axe to the roots of wickedness. He it is that poured wine on our wounded souls (the blood of David's vine), that brought the oil which flows from the compassions of the Father, and bestowed it copiously. He produced the ligatures of health and of salvation that cannot be undone, — Love, Faith, Hope.

Clement of Alexandria
c. 150-215

Several of Clement's writings have been lost throughout the ages but are referenced in some of his larger works. There are also a dozen treatises, which are attributed to Clement that are no longer exist.

SATURDAY, FOURTH WEEK OF LENT

Rule of Faith

For what I received I passed on to you as of first importance: that Christ died for our sins according to the Scriptures, that he was buried, that he was raised on the third day according to the Scriptures, and that he appeared to Peter, and then to the Twelve. After that, he appeared to more than five hundred of the brothers at the same time, most of whom are still living, though some have fallen asleep. Then he appeared to James, then to all the apostles, as to one abnormally born.

1 Corinthians 15:3-8

The Rule of Faith is altogether one, sole, immovable, and irreformable — namely, to believe in One God Almighty, the Maker of the world; and His Son, Jesus Christ, born of the Virgin Mary, crucified under Pontius Pilate, on the third day raised again from the dead, received in the heavens, sitting now at the right hand of the Father, coming to judge the quick and the dead, also through the resurrection of the flesh.

Tertullian

c. 160-225

Tertullian was raised in Carthage as a pagan and educated in literature and rhetoric. His full name is Quintus Septimius Florens Tertullian, and he practiced law before his conversion to Christ in 197 A.D. It is not sure if Tertullian was ordained or remained a layman. He did join the Montanist sect, which emphasized the Holy Spirit, the immediate Second Coming of Christ and perfectionism based in knowledge. He authored several works in Latin and Greek attacking pagan superstitions and promoting Christian morality. He challenged infant baptism and promoted the doctrine of original sin, which through Augustine came to dominate Roman theology. Tertullian upheld martyrdom as an important aspect in the faith and was probably the editor of the martyrdom of Perpetua and Felicitas.

FIFTH SUNDAY OF LENT

Standing Firm

*"I tell you the truth," Jesus replied, "no one who has left home
or brothers or sisters or mother or father or children or fields for me
and the gospel will fail to receive a hundred times as much in this
present age (homes, brothers, sisters, mothers, children and field —
and with them, persecutions) and in the age to come, eternal life."*
Mark 10:29-30

"While," says she, "we were still with the persecutors,
and my father, for the sake of his affection for me, was
persisting in seeking to turn me away, and to cast me down
from the faith, — 'Father,' said I, 'do you see, let us say, this
vessel lying here to be a little pitcher, or something else?' And
he said, 'I see it to be so.' And I replied to him, 'Can it be
called by any other name than what it is?' And he said, 'No.'
'Neither can I call my self anything else than what I am, a
Christian.' Then my father, provoked at this saying, threw
himself upon me, as if he would tear my eyes out. But he only
distressed me, and went away overcome by the devil's
arguments. Then, in a few days after I had been without my
father, I gave thanks to the Lord; and his absence became a
source of consolation to me. In that same interval of a few
days we were baptized, and to me the Spirit prescribed that in
the water *of baptism* nothing else was to be sought for than
bodily endurance.

Perpetua
d. 203

Perpetua and several African Christians were arrested after
their baptism and sentenced to be executed in the arena at
Carthage. Perpetua was born into a wealthy family and was
taught to read and write and had just given birth to an infant

son when she was arrested. Perpetua's servant Felicitas was also arrested when they were in a discipleship class with three men: Secundulus, Saturninus and Revocatus. They were charged with civil disobedience and refused to perform the Roman sacrifice of burning incense in honor of the emperor.

MONDAY, FIFTH WEEK OF LENT

Standing

Therefore put on the full armor of God, so that when the day of evil comes, you may be able to stand your ground, and after you have done everything, to stand.
Ephesians 6:13

And Hilarianus the procurator, who had just received the power of life and death in the place of the proconsul Minucius Timinianus, who was deceased, said, "Spare the grey hairs of your father, spare the infancy of your boy, offer sacrifice for the well-being of the emperors." And I replied, "I will not do so." Hilarianus said, "Are you a Christian?" And I replied, "I am a Christian." And as my father stood there to cast me down *from the faith,* he was ordered by Hilarianus to be thrown down, and was beaten with rods. And my father's misfortune grieved me as if I myself had been beaten, I so grieved for his wretched old age. The procurator then delivers judgment on all of us, and condemns us to the wild beasts, and we went down cheerfully to the dungeon. Then, because my child had been used to receive suck from me, and to stay with me in the prison, I send Pomponius the deacon to my father to ask for the infant, but my father would not give it him. And even as God willed it, the child no long desired the breast, nor did my breast cause me uneasiness, lest I should be tormented by care for my babe and by the pain of my breasts at once.
Perpetua
d. 203

A small group of new disciples were marched through Carthage on Caesar's birthday. Perpetua sang hymns of faith while the men shouted warnings to the people on the streets.

Felicitas gave birth to an infant girl days before the execution and was able to give her daughter to her sister. Two deacons from the church in Carthage witnessed the martyrdom and give their names as Tertius and Pomponius.

TUESDAY, FIFTH WEEK OF LENT

Remain Strong

Be joyful always; pray continually; give thanks in all circumstances, for this is God's will for you in Christ Jesus.
1 Thessalonians 5:16-18

Moreover, on the day before, when in that last meal, which they call the free meal, they were partaking as far as they could, not of a free supper, but of an *agape;* with the same firmness they were uttering such words as these to the people, denouncing *against them* the judgment of the Lord, bearing witness to the felicity of their passion, laughing at the curiosity of the people who came together; while Saturus said, "Tomorrow is not enough for you, for you to behold with pleasure that which you hate. Friends today, enemies tomorrow. Yet note our faces diligently, that you may recognize them on that day of judgment." Thus all departed thence astonished, and from these things many believed.

The day of their victory shone forth, and they proceeded from the prison into the amphitheatre, as if to an assembly, joyous and of brilliant countenances; if perchance shrinking, it was with joy, and not with fear. Perpetua followed with placid look, and with step and gait as a matron of Christ, beloved of God; casting down the luster of her eyes from the gaze of all. Moreover, Felicitas, rejoicing that she had safely brought forth, so that she might fight with the wild beasts; from the blood and from the midwife to the gladiator.

Perpetua
d. 203

The believers were mauled by wild beasts, including a mad cow that was let into the arena. Gladiators dragged the Christians before the crowds and then proceeded to cut open their throats. Before this final act of violence it was noted that the Christian martyrs kissed each other as a sign of peace. Perpetua, groaning and in great pain, guided the gladiator's trembling hand to her own throat. Her last recorded words were to her brother who was also a new Christian: "Remain strong in your faith and love one another. Do not let our excruciating suffering become a stumbling block for you."

WEDNESDAY, FIFTH WEEK OF LENT

Conquering Faith

How, then, can they call on the one they have not believed in?
And how can they believe in the one of whom they have not heard?
And how can they hear without someone preaching to them? And
how can they preach unless they are sent? As it is written, "How
beautiful are the feet of those who bring good news!"
Romans 10:14-17

How beautiful is the spectacle to God when a Christian
does battle with pain; when he is drawn up against threats,
and punishments, and tortures; when, mocking the noise of
death, he treads under foot the horror of the executioner;
when he raises up his liberty against kings and princes, and
yields to God alone, whose he is; when, triumphant and
victorious, he tramples upon the very man who has pro-
nounced sentence again him! For he has conquered who has
obtained that for which he contends. What soldier would not
provoke peril with greater boldness under the eyes of his
general? For no one receives a reward before his trial, and
yet the general does not give what he has not: he cannot
preserve life, but he can make the warfare glorious. But
God's soldier is neither forsaken in suffering, nor is brought
to an end by death. Thus the Christian may seem to be
miserable; he cannot be really found to be so.

Minucius Felix
c. 250-311

Minucius Felix was an African Christian who wrote in Latin a
conversation between Octavius the Christian and Calecilius.
He argues for monotheism and the grace of God upon all
people. He also defends Christianity against the persecutions
being false charges that were attributed to them, such as

rioters, disease spreaders, revilers and dissenters. Some historians believe this work to be connected to Tertullian's "Apology," which was written around 197.

THURSDAY, FIFTH WEEK OF LENT

Christ Crucified

Where is the wise man? Where is the scholar? Where is the philosopher of this age? Has not God made foolish the wisdom of the world? For since in the wisdom of God the world through its wisdom did not know him, God was pleased through the foolishness of what was preached to save those who believe. Jews demand miraculous signs and Greeks look for wisdom, but we preach Christ crucified: a stumbling block to Jews and foolishness to Gentiles, but to those whom God has called, both Jews and Greeks, Christ the power of God and the wisdom of God.
1 Corinthians 1:20-24

I have spoken of the twofold sign whence death proceeded, and again I have said that thence life frequently proceeds; but the cross has become foolishness to an adulterous people. The awful King of eternity shadows forth *these things* by the cross, that they may now believe on Him. O fools, that live in death! Cain slew his younger brother by the invention of the wickedness. Thence the sons of Enoch are said to be the race of Cain. Then the evil people increased in the world, which never transfers souls to God. To believe the cross came to be a dread, and they say that they live righteously. The first law was in the tree; and thence, too, the second. And thence the second law first of all overcame the terrible law with peace. Lifted up, they have rushed into vain prevarication. They are unwilling to acknowledge the Lord pierced with nails; but when His judgment shall come, they will then discern Him. But the race of Abel already believes on a merciful Christ.

Commodianus
d. 240

Commondianus was a North African Christian whose writings consist of two poems that have survived.

FRIDAY, FIFTH WEEK OF LENT

One Lord

And being found in appearance as a man, he humbled himself and became obedient to death — even death on a cross! Therefore God exalted him to the highest place and gave him the name that is above every name, that at the name of Jesus every knee should bow, in heaven and on earth and under the earth, and every tongue confess that Jesus Christ is Lord, to the glory of God the Father.
Philippians 2:8-11

Seeing, then, that such is the end, when all enemies will be subdued to Christ, when death — the last enemy — shall be destroyed, and when the kingdom shall be delivered up by Christ (to whom all things are subject) to God the Father; let us, I say, from such an end as this, contemplate the beginnings of things. For the end is always like the beginning: and, therefore, as there is one end to all things, so ought we to understand that there was one beginning; and as there is one end to many things, so there spring from one beginning many differences and varieties, which again, through the goodness of God, and by subjection to Christ, and through the unity of the Holy Spirit, are recalled to one end, which is like unto the beginning: all those, viz., who, bending the knee at the name of Jesus, make known by so doing their subjection to Him.

Origen
c. 185-254

Origen was born in Egypt and was raised in a Christian home with his father being martyred when he was 17 years old. He wrote commentaries on most of the Bible and contributed to a systematic study of God. Most of his theological works are lost, but many of his sermons and letters still exist. He was arrested and tortured for being a Christian and died in prison.

SATURDAY, FIFTH WEEK OF LENT

Visible Faith

For it is shameful even to mention what the disobedient do in secret. But everything exposed by the light becomes visible, for it is light that makes everything visible. This is why it is said: "Wake up, O sleeper, rise from the dead, and Christ will shine on you." Be very careful, then, how you live — not as unwise but as wise, making the most of every opportunity, because the days are evil. Therefore do not be foolish, but understand what the Lord's will is.
Ephesians 5:12-17

The rule of truth demands that, first of all, we believe in God the Father and Almighty Lord, that is, the most perfect *Maker of all things* ... The same rule of truth teaches us to believe, after the Father, also in the son of God, Christ Jesus, our Lord God, but the Son of God ... . Moreover, the order of reason and the authority of faith, in due consideration of the words and Scriptures of the Lord, admonishes us, after this, to *believe* also in the Holy Ghost, promised of old to the Church, but granted in the appointed and fitting time.

Novatian of Rome
c. 250

Novatian was an elder and eventually a bishop of Rome in the middle of the third century. He questioned the discipline concerning those who forsook the faith and then wanted to be readmitted into the church. The above confession is more than a baptismal formula because of its emphasis on the authority of faith that accompanies the confession of faith. Later on Novatian would include in his articles of religious section on the holy church, the remission of sins and the resurrection of Jesus Christ.

PALM SUNDAY

Humiliation

A very large crowd spread their cloaks on the road, while others cut branches from the trees and spread them on the road. The crowds that went ahead of him and those that followed shouted, "Hosanna to the Son of David!" "Blessed is he who comes in the name of the Lord!" "Hosanna in the highest!" When Jesus entered Jerusalem, the whole city was stirred and asked, "Who is this?" The crowds answered, "This is Jesus, the prophet from Nazareth in Galilee."
Matthew 21:8-11

He has no form nor glory; and we beheld Him, and He had not any form nor beauty: but His appearance was without honour, and deficient more than that of all men. He was a man under suffering, and who knew how to bear sickness: because His countenance was averted, He was treated with disrespect, and was made of no account. This man bears our sins, and suffers pain on our behalf; and we reguarded Him a sin trouble, and in suffering, and as ill-treated. But He was wounded for our sins, and bruised for our iniquities. The chastisement of our peace was upon Him; by His stripes we were healed. We all, like sheep, wandered from the way. A man wandered in his way, and the Lord delivered Him on account of our sins; and He, because of His evil treatment, opens not His mouth. As a sheep was He led to slaughter; and as a lamb before her shearer is dumb, so He opens not His mouth. In His humiliation His judgment was taken away.
Origen
c. 185-254

Origen was not without controversy. He always directed his prayers to Jesus Christ only; he believed in a finite God, practiced a form of mysticism and flirted with universalism. The difficulty with Origen is the loss of most of his original works and therefore an unsatisfactory analysis.

HOLY MONDAY

Water and Spirit

In reply Jesus declared, "I tell you the truth, no one can see the kingdom of God unless he is born again." "How can a man be born when he is old?" Nicodmus asked, "Surely he cannot enter a second time into his mother's womb to be born!" Jesus answered, "I tell you the truth, no one can enter the kingdom of God unless he is born of water and the Spirit. Flesh gives birth to flesh, but the Spirit gives birth to spirit."
John 3:3-6

The Father of immortality sent the immortal Son and Word into the world, who came to man in order to wash him with water and the Spirit; and He, begetting us again to the breath (spirit) of life, and endued us with an incorruptible panoply. If, therefore, man has become immortal, he will also be God. And if he is made God by water and the Holy Spirit after the regeneration of the layer he is found to be also joint-heir with Christ after the resurrection from the dead. Wherefore I preach to this effect: Come, all ye kindreds of the nations, to the immortality of the baptism. I bring good tidings of life to you who tarry in the darkness of ignorance. Come into liberty from slavery, into a kingdom from tyranny, into incorruption from corruption. And how, saith one, shall we come? How? By water and the Holy Ghost.

Hippolytus
c.170-236

Hippolytus was probably the most important theologian of the third century because he often wrote in the Greek language. He was elected bishop of Rome but never claimed to be pope. Hippolytus' main contribution was his defense of the orthodox faith along with commentaries on the Old Testament.
Hippoytus heard a sermon by Origen in Rome and spent most of his life in Italy.

HOLY TUESDAY

The Struggle of Faith

*You must be on your guard. You will be handed over to the
local councils and flogged in the synagogues. On account of me
you will stand before governors and kings as witnesses to them.
And the gospel must first be preached to all nations. Whenever
you are arrested and brought to trial, do not worry beforehand
about what to say. Just say whatever is given you at the time, for it
is not you speaking, but the Holy Spirit.*
Mark 13:9-11

When we read these things, and things of the like kind,
brought together in the Gospel, and feel, as it were, torches
placed under us, with the Lord's words to inflame our faith,
we not only do not dread, but we even provoke the enemies
of the truth; and we have already conquered the opponents
of God, by the very fact of our not yielding to them, and
have subdued their nefarious laws against the truth. And
although we have not yet shed our blood, we are prepared
to shed it. Let no one think that this delay of our departure is
any clemency; for it obstructs us, it makes a hindrance to our
glory, it puts off heaven, it withholds the glorious sight of
God. For in a contest of this kind, and in the kind of contest
when faith is struggling in the encounter, it is not true
clemency to put off martyrs by delay.

Cyprian
d.258

Cyprian was the bishop of Carthage in North Africa who
studied under Tertullian. He was converted to Christianity in
246 from a life of teaching, rhetoric and logic. During the
persecution of the Roman Emperor Valerian, Cyprian was
arrested and martyred in September 258. He was known for his
charitable works, including serving those who were dying of
the plague.

HOLY WEDNESDAY

Established in the Faith

I tell you the truth, this generation will certainly not pass away until all these things have happened. Heaven and earth will pass away, but my words will never pass away. Be careful, or your hearts will be weighed down with dissipation, drunkenness and the anxieties of life, and that day will close on you unexpectedly like a trap. For it will come upon all those who live on the face of the whole earth. Be always on the watch, and pray that you may be able to escape all that is about to happen, and that you may be able to stand before the Son of Man.
Luke 21:32-36

Which things must all now be considered by us, that no one may desire anything from the world that is now dying, but may follow Christ, who both lives for ever, and quickens His servants, who are established in the faith of His name. For there comes the time, beloved brethren, which our Lord long ago foretold and taught us was approaching, saying, "The time cometh, that whosoever killeth you will think that he doeth God service. And these things they will do unto you, because they have not known the Father nor me. But these things have I told you, that when the time shall come, ye may remember that I told you of them." Nor let any one wonder that we are harassed with constant persecutions, and continually tried with increasing afflictions, when the Lord before predicted that these things would happen in the last times, and has instructed us for the warfare by the teaching and exhortation of His words.

Cyprian
d. 258

Cyprian's writings include letters and sermons on apologetics, virginity and unity within the body of Christ. As a located bishop, he pastored a local church and wrote on very practical matters rather than speculative, theological ones.

MAUNDY THURSDAY

Facing Temptation

He withdrew about a stone's throw beyond them, knelt down and prayed, "Father, if you are willing, take this cup from me; yet not my will, but yours be done."
Luke 22:41-42

But let these things be enough to say on the subject of the will. This word, however, "Let the cup pass," does not mean, "Let it not come near me, or approach me." For what can pass from Him must certainly first come nigh Him, and what does thus pass from Him must be by Him. For if it does not reach Him, it cannot pass from Him. Accordingly, as if He now felt it to be present, He began to be in pain, and to be troubled, and to be sore amazed, and to be in agony. And as if it was at hand and placed before Him He does not merely say "the cup," but He indicates it by the word "this." Therefore, as what passes from one is something which neither has no approach nor is permanently settled with one, so the Saviour's first request is that the temptation which has come softly and plainly upon Him and associated itself lightly with Him, may be turned aside. And this is the first form of that freedom from falling into temptation, which He also counsels the weaker disciples to make the subject of their prayers; that, namely, which concerns the approach of temptation: for it must needs be that offences come, but yet those to whom they come ought not to fall into the temptation. But the most perfect mode in which this freedom from entering into temptation is exhibited, is what He expresses in His second request, when He says not merely, "Not as I will," but also, "but as Thou wilt."

Dionysuis the Great
d. 264

Dionysuis was bishop of Alexandria and spent most of his life facing Roman persecution.

GOOD FRIDAY

Between Earth and Heaven

*When the centurion and those with him who were guarding Jesus
saw the earthquake and all that had happened, they were terrified, and
exclaimed, "Surely he was the Son of God!" Many women were there,
watching from a distance. They had followed Jesus from Galilee to care
for his needs. Among them were Mary Magdalene, Mary the mother
of James and Joses, and the mother of Zebedee's sons.*
Matthew 27:54-56

For the Word suffered, being in the flesh affixed to the
cross, that He might bring man, who had been deceived by
error, to His supreme and godlike majesty, restoring him to
that divine life from which he had become alienated. By this
figure, in truth, the passions are blunted; the passion of the
passions having taken place by the Passion, and the death of
death by the death of Christ, He not having been subdued
by death, nor overcome by the pains of the Passion. For
neither did the Passion cast Him down from His equanimity,
nor did death hurt Him, but He was in the passible remaining, and in the mortal remaining immortal, comprehending
all that the air and this middle state, and the heaven above
contained, and attempering the mortal to the immortal
divinity. Death was vanquished entirely; the flesh being
crucified to draw forth its immortality.

Methodius of Olympus
d. 311

Methodius was bishop of Olympus and Patara and eventually
oversaw churches in Phoenicia. He suffered martyrdom in
Greece and died defending his faith. He was known as the
antagonist of Origen and wrote mostly on virginity, resurrection
and eternal life. The only complete work of Methodius to
survive is *The Banquet of the Ten Virgins,* which is a dialogue on
the power and grace of God. At the end of this writing there is a
hymn dedicated to Jesus Christ as the bridegroom of the church.

HOLY SATURDAY

Life in Christ

*For Christ died for sins once for all, the righteous for the
unrighteous, to bring you to God. He was put to death in the body
but made alive by the Spirit, through whom also he went and
preached to the spirits in prison who disobeyed long ago when God
waited patiently in the days of Noah while the ark was being built.
In it only a few people, eight in all, were saved through water, and
this water symbolizes baptism that now saves you also – not the
removal of dirt from the body but the pledge of a good conscience
toward God.*
1 Peter 3:18-21

He, who was not man, became man, that "as in Adam all
die, even so in Christ shall all be made alive." For if He bore
flesh for any other reason than that of setting the flesh free,
and raising it up, why did He bear flesh superfluously, as He
purposed neither to save it, nor to raise it up? But the Son of
God does nothing superfluously. He did not then take the
form of a servant uselessly, but to raise it up and save it. For
He truly was made man, and died, and not in mere appearance, but that He might truly be shown to be the first
begotten from the dead, changing the earthy into the heavenly, and the mortal into the immortal. When, then, Paul
says that "flesh and blood cannot inherit the kingdom of
God." He does not give a disparaging opinion of the regeneration of the flesh, but would teach that the kingdom of
God, which is eternal life, is not possessed by the body, but
the body by the life.
Methodius of Olympus
d. 311

Methodius defended human liberty against the Gnostics by
writing a treatise on free will.

RESURECTION SUNDAY

Remember

Praise be to the God and Father of our Lord Jesus Christ! In his great mercy he has given us new birth into a living hope through the resurrection of Jesus Christ from the dead.
1 Peter 1:3

There is one God, the Father of living Word, *who is His* subsistent Wisdom and Power and Eternal Image: perfect Begetter of the perfect *Begotten,* Father of the only-begotten Son. There is one Lord, Only of the Only, God of God, Image and Likeness of Deity, Efficient Word, Wisdom comprehensive of the Constitution of all things, and Power formative of the whole creation, true Son of true Father, Invisible of Invisible, and Incorruptible of Incorruptible, and Immortal of Immortal, and Eternal of Eternal. And there is One Holy Spirit, having His subsistence from God, and being made manifest by the Son, to wit to men: Image of the Son, Perfect *Image* of the Perfect; Life, the Cause of the living; Holy Fount; Sanctity, the Supplier, *or Leader* of Sanctification; in whom is manifested God the Father, who is above all and in all, and God the Son, who is through all. There is a perfect Trinity, in glory and eternity and sovereignty, neither divided nor estranged. Wherefore there is nothing either created or in servitude in the Trinity; nor anything super induced, as if at some former period it was non-existent, and at some later period it was introduced. And thus neither was the Son ever wanting to the Father, nor the Spirit to the Son; but without variation and without change, the same Trinity *abideth* ever.

Gregory Thaumaturgus
c. 205-265

Gregory was raised in the polytheism of Greece and was converted on a journey to Palestine in 233. He became a disciple of Origen and was made bishop of Pontus. His last name came be translated "wonder worker," which testifies to his strength of character and abundance of compassion.

EASTER MONDAY

Productive Lives

Our people must learn to devote themselves to doing what is good, in order that they may provide for daily necessities and not live unproductive lives. Everyone with me sends you greetings. Greet those who love us in the faith. Grace be with you all.
Titus 3:14-15

The faithful of Christ, therefore, remembering all this with pious devotion, brought his sacred body, and caused it to sit upon the Episcopal throne. As much joy and exultation arose then to heaven from the people, as if they were attending him alive and in the body. Then embalming him with sweet spices, they wrapped him in silken coverings; what each one of them could be the first to bring, this he accounted to himself as greatest gain. Then carrying palms, the tokens of victory, with flaming tapers, with sounding hymns, and with fragrant incense, celebrating the triumph of his heavenly victory, they laid down the sacred relics, and buried them in the cemetery which had been long ago constructed by him, where too from henceforth, and even to this day, miraculous virtues cease not to show themselves. Pious vows, forsooth, are received with a propitious hearing; the health of the impotent is restored; the expulsion of unclean spirits testifies to the martyr's merits. These gifts, O Lord Jesus, are Thine, whose wont it is thus magnificently to honour Thy martyrs after death: Thou who with the Father and the Holy Consubstantial Spirit livest and reignest for evermore. Amen.

Peter Bishop of Alexandria
c. 260-311

Peter is remembered for his holy living and his knowledge of the Scriptures. He survived one persecution while hiding in the wilderness but secured his fate by returning to his flock and meeting death by the sword. Very little of his writings remain, and this particular passage deals with piety and passion.

BIBLIOGRAPHY

Roberts, Alexander, D.D., Donaldson, James, LL.D. *The Writings of the Fathers Down to A.D. 325, Volume 1 The Apostolic Fathers.* Peabody, Massachusetts: Hendrickson Publishing, Inc., 1994.

Roberts, Alexander, D.D., Donaldson, James, LL.D. *The Writings of the Fathers Down to A.D. 325, Volume 2 Fathers of the Second Century.* Peabody, Massachusetts: Hendrickson Publishing, Inc., 1994.

Roberts, Alexander, D.D., Donaldson, James, LL.D. *The Writings of the Fathers Down to A.D. 325, Volume 3 Turtullian (I, II, III).* Peabody, Massachusetts: Hendrickson Publishing, Inc., 1994.

Roberts, Alexander, D.D., Donaldson, James, LL.D. *The Writings of the Fathers Down to A.D. 325, Volume 4 Turtullian (IV), Minucius Felix, Commondian, Origen.* Peabody, Massachusetts: Hendrickson Publishing, Inc., 1994.

Roberts, Alexander, D.D., Donaldson, James, LL.D. *The Writings of the Fathers Down to A.D. 325 Ante-Nicene Fathers, Volume 5 Hippolytus, Cyprian, Caius, Novatian.* Peabody, Massachusetts: Hendrickson Publishing, Inc., 1994.

Roberts, Alexander, D.D., Donaldson, James, LL.D. *The Writings of the Fathers Down to A.D. 325, Volume 6 Gregory Thaumaturgus, Dionysius the Great, Julius Africanus, Anatoolius and Minor Wrtiers, Methodius, Arnobius.* Peabody, Massachusetts: Hendrickson Publishing, Inc., 1994.

Schaff, Philip. *The Creeds of Christendom Volume 1.* Grand Rapids: Baker Books, 1993.

LaVergne, TN USA
12 February 2010
172905LV00001B/1/P